# CONTENTS:2006

# CHAMPIONS AGAIN

## The 2004/05 SPL Season

AUGUST 2004

**07.08.04:  Aberdeen 0 Rangers 0**
For the opening fixture of the 2004/05 league campaign, Rangers travelled north to face Aberdeen with new signings Gregory Vignal (French), Jean-Alain Boumsong (French), Alex Rae (Scottish), Nacho Novo (Spanish) and Dado Prso (Croatian) all in the starting line-up.  Despite creating chances in each half and hitting the bar, the visitors failed to break the deadlock and the match ended 0-0.

**14.08.04:  Rangers 4 Livingston 0**
Marvin Andrews was in the starting eleven against his former club Livingston as Rangers cruised to victory with two goals in either half.  A Prso shot from close range opened the scoring before Stephen Hughes doubled the advantage, netting from Peter Lovenkrands' penalty box drive.  After the break, Rangers' domination continued and Hughes claimed his second after substitute Steven Thompson misfired in front of goal.  Then, right at the end, Shota Arveladze drilled home a powerful shot from inside the area.

**21.08.04:  Rangers 4 Hibernian 1**
Although Hibernian (managed by ex-Celt Tony Mowbray) provided a sterner test at Ibrox the following week, rampant Rangers hit four goals for the second time in two games.  Early-on, it looked as if Hibernian were in for a real hammering, losing two in the first fifteen minutes of play with both Arveladze and then Prso finding the net with headers.  Even at this early stage of his career in Scotland, it was obvious that Prso had developed a strong bond with the Ibrox crowd.  Caldwell closed the gap for the visitors late in the first-half but Boumsong's powerful header (from a Vignal corner) made it 3-1 before Lovenkrands burst through late-on to rifle past Simon Brown in goal.  Match mascot on the day was a certain young lad with the delightful name of Oleg Kuznetsov Singh!

**29.08.04: Celtic 1 Rangers 0**
Despite performing well in the east end of the city, Rangers were beaten by a late Alan Thompson strike just when it seemed as if they would be returning to Govan with a well earned draw.  The harsh reality however was that Rangers were now five points behind after just four league games.

SEPTEMBER 2004

**12.09.04:  Hearts 0 Rangers 0**
For the third time in three away league games this season, Rangers failed to find the back of the net after a bruising encounter with Hearts at Tynecastle ended 0-0.  There was now a seven point gap between fourth place Rangers and leaders Celtic.

**19.09.04:  Rangers 1 Inverness CT 0**
Although all three points were secured the following week after a tight 1-0 home victory over Inverness, it was

# THE OFFICIAL
# RANGERS FOOTBALL CLUB
## ANNUAL 2006

Written by Douglas Russell

Designed by Colin Heggie

A Grange Publication

© 2005. Published by Grange Communications Ltd., Edinburgh, under licence from The Rangers Football Club plc. Printed in the EU.

ISBN 1-902704-97-5

obvious Rangers were far from firing on all cylinders. Defender Boumsong struck woodwork before and after the break but it was a first half headed goal from Dado Prso that actually separated the sides. This was the Croatian's third of the season, with all three of the striker's goals scored on Govan soil.

## 26.09.04: Dundee 0 Rangers 2

Nacho Novo answered his critics in quite devastating style when, after replacing Arveladze midway through the second period of the game against Dundee at Dens Park, the little Spaniard scored twice against his old club. The goals in the 2-0 victory (the first from close-in with his left foot and the second a right-foot drive from just inside the penalty area) came in the space of three minutes following good play, on both occasions, by winger Chris Burke.

# OCTOBER 2004

## 3.10.04: Rangers 2 Kilmarnock 0

Novo (with a great finish) scored again the following Sunday as Rangers hit another two without reply when Kilmarnock came calling. Without doubt, however, the man of the match was hulking defender Marvin Andrews who claimed his first goal for the club and, indeed, might have had a hat-trick before the final whistle and another long journey to the Caribbean on international duty.

## 17.10.04: Motherwell 0 Rangers 2

For the third SPL clash in a row that 2-0 winning sequence continued. Stefan Klos was again magnificent in goal and Dado Prso's double (one in each half) meant all three points at Fir Park against Motherwell. The striker's first, in seven minutes, was a delightful chip over Marshall after a super run following Fernando Ricksen's feed from midfield. His second, just seven minutes before the end of the ninety, was a powerful low drive after good work by both Ricksen and Novo.

## 24.10.04: Ranger 1 Dundee United 1

It looked as if Nacho Novo's stunning 20-yard strike would be enough but former Ibrox youth Barry Robson netted with a free-kick right at the end to steal a draw for his side. Despite the fact that it was a marvellous strike, it was a cruel blow indeed and the first goal that Stefan Klos had lost in the league since the end of August.

**31.10.04: Rangers 5 Aberdeen 0**
Having beaten Celtic in Glasgow only four days earlier, a confident Aberdeen travelled to Ibrox in the belief that a second Old Firm scalp in one week was a realistic possibility. They returned north, however, in a slightly different frame of mind after a 5-0 Hallowe'en humiliation! Substitute Steven Thompson (on for Prso who needed eight stitches in a head wound after a clash with defender Severin) claimed the close range opener late in the first half before the flood gates opened in the second period with goals from Peter Lovenkrands, Nacho Novo (a double to take his tally to eight in eight games) and Fernando Ricksen.

## NOVEMBER 2004

**7.11.04: Livingston 1 Rangers 4**
Alex McLeish's men extended their unbeaten run in all competitions to eleven matches (ten victories and a draw) with an impressive 4-1 triumph to maintain the pressure on Celtic. At Almondvale, Lovenkrands' first-half conversion was followed by another trio in the second forty-five courtesy of Novo, Thompson and Hamed Namouchi.

**14.11.04: Hibernian 0 Rangers 1**
Four days after beating Celtic in the CIS Cup quarter-final, Rangers travelled east along the M8 to Edinburgh for an Easter Road meeting with Hibernian. Less than half an hour into the game, the harsh dismissal of Novo made the Light Blues' task difficult in the extreme but a second-half performance full of character was more than enough to secure a crucial victory. Dado Prso, with his eighth since arriving from Monaco, netted from the penalty spot after a foul on Namouchi had led to Caldwell's dismissal.

**20.11.04: Rangers 2 Celtic 0**
For consecutive matches, Rangers were involved in a game that saw two players sent-off. This time, however, they were both wearing green. Any encounter with old friends Celtic is usually a meaty affair but this Ibrox clash was of the X certificate variety. Novo opened the scoring from the penalty spot after the wee man had been scythed down in the box by Valgaeren before Prso doubled the advantage in 36 minutes with a superb header from Ricksen's inviting free kick into the area. Shortly after, the visitors were down to ten men when Thompson was shown red for aiming a head-butt at Peter Lovenkrands. Sutton was the next Celt to be dismissed following a second yellow card offence after the break. Rangers played out the game comfortably and, for the first time since Martin O'Neill had taken charge, kept a clean sheet against Celtic.

**28.11.04: Rangers 3 Hearts 2**
At the end of a November to remember, Rangers took pole position in the league. With their great rivals drawing at Dens Park, this 3-2 defeat of Hearts ensured top spot in the SPL for the first time since October 2003 - more than a year earlier. A Nacho Novo brace (for a total of 13 goals in his last 14 games) and a McAllister own-goal (as Ricksen challenged for a Lovenkrands ball into the six yard area) earned the points despite John Robertson's side having taken a fifteen-minute lead in the game.

## DECEMBER 2004

**5.12.04: Inverness CT 1 Rangers 1**
The month began with a disappointing 1-1 draw in the game with Caley Thistle at Pittodrie. Although Dado Prso

equalised early in the second period (the home side had gone ahead with just three minutes on the clock), Rangers could not find the winner.

### 11.12.04: Rangers 3 Dundee 0

With Alex McLeish celebrating three years in charge at the club, any lingering memories of the previous week's poor showing up north were banished within three minutes of the start of this game. By that early stage, Rangers were already two ahead courtesy of Novo's penalty and Prso's fiercely drilled shot. Just after the interval, the home fans acclaimed a quite stunning strike by Bob Malcolm from outside the box to make the final score 3-0.

### 19.12.04: Kilmarnock 0 Rangers 1

Shota Arveladze, a replacement for the suspended Nacho Novo, claimed the only goal on a bitter Ayrshire afternoon with a rifled shot in sixteen minutes. Having accumulated 38 points out of a possible 42 from their last fourteen games, the players certainly deserved some Christmas celebrations.

### 27.12.04: Rangers 4 Motherwell 1

Taking his season's tally to 17, Novo hit a double in the 4-1 Glasgow beating of Motherwell. His first, for the second home game in a row, was netted after just two minutes of play. Then, on the fifteen-minute mark, his theme tune was blaring through the loudspeakers again after he raced on to an Arveladze through-ball and buried past Corr. Although McDonald pulled one back for Terry Butcher's young side, Arveladze made it 3-1 at the break before substitute Steven Thompson completed the scoring just in advance of the final whistle.

JANUARY 2005

### 15.1.05: **Rangers 3 Dunfermline 0**

A comfortable win over the Fifers was just the tonic that Rangers needed after exiting the Scottish Cup at the hands of Celtic the previous week. Steven Thompson claimed his seventh of an injury-hit campaign early on before man of the match Marvin Andrews doubled the advantage (his second in Rangers' colours) with a shot from a crowded penalty area. Perhaps the happiest player on the entire park, however, was Alex Rae whose first-ever goal for his boyhood heroes obviously meant so much to the midfielder.

### 23.1.05: **Aberdeen 1 Rangers 2**

Rangers 300th meeting with Aberdeen ended in another victory. After Prso had fired his side ahead in eight minutes, home keeper Ryan Esson, with a helping hand, somehow pushed the ball into his own net from Ricksen's corner and it was suddenly 2-0 to Rangers. Mackie pulled one back (Aberdeen's first SPL goal in 432 minutes of league football!) but McLeish's eleven held firm for another satisfying three points.

### 1.1.05: **Dundee United 1 Rangers 1**

All seemed lost at Tannadice before goalkeeper Stefan Klos caused mayhem in the Dundee United box when his arrival for a last minute corner enabled Hamed Namouchi to bundle home for a share of the points. The home side had led from the 11th minute against a Rangers side now minus Boumsong after his £8 million transfer to Newcastle in the Premiership.

### 29.1.05: **Rangers 3 Livingston 0**

Greek central defender Sotirios Kyrgiakos strolled faultlessly through his Rangers debut and even set up Prso for the first goal of the game. Second half strikes from both Ricksen (a wicked free-kick into the top corner) and Novo ensured a straightforward win on the day that legend Richard Gough returned to Ibrox but this time in his new role as the visitors' manager.

## FEBRUARY 2005

### 12.2.05: Rangers 3 Hibernian 0
Before this Ibrox clash, Hibernian had put together an impressive unbeaten eight-match run. On the day, however, they were simply outclassed and really rather fortunate to return to the capital nursing only a 3-0 hangover. With Barry Ferguson back in the fold and pulling the midfield strings, the fans witnessed one of the best performances of the season from their favourites who made 17 attempts on goal including a missed Novo penalty. Prso netted in both halves (a header and a left-foot drive) and new boy Thomas Buffel followed up his midweek CIS Cup goal with a well-taken strike. Dutch goalkeeper Ronald Waterreus made his home debut.

### 20.2.05: Celtic 0 Rangers 2
Five years of Celtic Park pain finally came to an end with this famous 2-0 win in the east end of Glasgow. Although Celtic controlled the first half, watertight Waterreus just would not be beaten and he kept Rangers from going behind on more than one occasion. The Light Blues dominated after the break and goals from Gregory Vignal (a long range shot fumbled by Douglas that was Rangers 200th Old Firm league goal) and Nacho Novo (a delightful lob over the keeper) sent the inhabitants of one particular corner of the ground into blue heaven. It was one of those special days for all friends of the club.

### 26.2.05: Rangers 2 Kilmarnock 1
The twin terrors Prso and Novo both scored in this 2-1 victory but Alan Hutton's leg break cast a dark shadow over the day's proceedings. The Croatian's opener was a majestic 25-yard strike that arched over Combe in

goal whilst the Spaniard's 17th league goal of the season was a piece of opportunism after a slack pass back to the keeper by Ford.

## MARCH 2005

### 2.3.05: Hearts 1 Rangers 2
After a poor first-half showing at Tynecastle, Rangers seemed to have control of the clash with Hearts following Novo's beautifully taken opener early in the second period. Striking partner Prso's subsequent lob over Gordon deserved to double the visitor's tally but it was cleared off the line. The Gorgie side, however, equalised late on when ex-Celt Burchill tapped home after a Hartley free kick came off the post. In added time, chaos ensued when the linesman flagged for a foul on Kyrgiakos in the box and referee Dallas understandably awarded a spot-kick. Ricksen, with a thunderous drive, made no mistake to ensure a controversial end to the game.

### 5.3.05: Rangers 1 Inverness CT 1
On a cold day, this disappointing home draw with Inverness did little to warm the fans and handed the title initiative back to Celtic. Barry Ferguson's first goal since his return to Glasgow looked to be just enough but it was cancelled outright at the end when some amateurish defending enabled Prunty to equalise. Eight valuable points had now been dropped in the four games with Inverness and Dundee United.

### 13.3.05: Dundee 0 Rangers 2
With no shots at all on target throughout the whole of the opening forty-five, Rangers left it late at Dens Park as the pressure mounted. With less than ten minutes to play, Marvin Andrews was

the hero who broke the deadlock. His powerful penalty box header was complemented almost immediately by Ricksen's close range finish after fine control by Prso in the lead up play to that second goal.

### 3.4.05: Motherwell 2 Rangers 3
In their first match after that Hampden CIS Cup mauling two weeks earlier, Motherwell naturally looked to make amends. However, after a first-half double from Gregory Vignal (the first of which was a glorious right-foot drive high past Marshall), the visitors were well in control. It certainly seemed to be all over when Prso made it 3-0 with a glancing header six minutes after the restart but Butcher's men grabbed two in reply to ensure a pulsating end to the game. Rangers had earlier been reduced to ten men following the dismissal of Barry Ferguson when he reacted with anger to a bad tackle from substitute Foran and received his second yellow card of the game. With Celtic having lost at home to Hearts the previous day, Rangers now led the table by one precious point.

### 12.4.05: Rangers 0 Dundee United 1
Only three days after beating Hibernian in the semi-final of the Scottish Cup, bottom of the league Dundee United became the first SPL team to win at Ibrox this season. Certainly Rangers had plenty of chances following United's early strike but some dreadful finishing allied to great defending (particularly from goalkeeper Bullock) ensured the most unlikely of championship results.

### 17.4.05: Dunfermline 0 Rangers 1
In the final game before the league split, Rangers travelled to Dunfermline and came home with all three points thanks to Dado Prso's early-headed goal, his 19th of the season.

### 24.4.05: Rangers 1 Celtic 2
After a poor first-half showing (Celtic were 2-0 to the good at the interval), Rangers certainly stepped up a gear in the second period and created several goalscoring opportunities. However, Steven Thompson's late penalty box strike was all they had to show for their efforts and, with only four games left, title hopes seemed to be fading.

### 1.5.05: Aberdeen 1 Rangers 3
No doubt galvanised by the fact that the championship was still in the balance (leaders Celtic had been beaten at home by Hibernian the previous day), Rangers were at their impressive best at Pittodrie with one of the displays of the season. Barry Ferguson opened the scoring with a superbly taken left-foot shot on the run after being fed by Dado Prso from wide. Although Clark equalised, with the aid of a deflection, Rangers remained in control and two further goals from Dado sealed an important win. His first, a classic back heel into the net, was complemented in the 60th minute with a spin and shot from close range following an Andrews knock-down.

### 7.5.05: Rangers 2 Hearts 1
Thomas Buffel, playing just behind lone striker Dado Prso, was the man of the match in a game that was never as close as the final score suggested. The Belgian claimed Rangers' first before the ten minute mark with a neat header after Nacho Novo's initial shot had been cleared off the line by Webster. Buffel was also involved for the second when

Marvin Andrews deflected his 18-yard shot high into the net past Gordon between the posts. Hearts rarely threatened and their goal, near the end, came as a result of Andrews' outstretched leg which turned a rather harmless Stewart free kick into the net.

## 14.5.05: Rangers 4 Motherwell 1

Shota Arveladze, playing his last home game for the club, and Thomas Buffel both netted twice in a one-sided match that featured 13 Rangers shots on target compared to none for the Motherwell opposition. Once again, Belgian Buffel was quite superb and opened the scoring with a right foot shot past Marshall after having sped away from young defender Kinniburgh.

Four minutes later, Arveladze made it two by burying, from ten yards, Dado Prso's ball into the area. Shota, early in the second period, notched his second following a blistering run down the right flank by Nacho Novo who then 'laid it on a plate' for the Georgian before number four from Buffel – a powerful drive into the bottom corner after being set up by Prso. An Andrews OG right at the end was Motherwell's only consolation.

## 22.5.05 Hibernian 0 Rangers 1

Nacho Novo, with his first goal since CIS Cup Final day back in late March, hit the winner with just over thirty minutes left to play. Following good combination work by Prso and Buffel, the Spaniard's 25th of the season was a fiercely driven, low shot from the right that beat keeper Brown for the only goal of the game. Rangers knew that winning at Easter Road would not be enough to take the title - Celtic had to drop points at Fir Park as well. Sensationally, right at the end of their fixture, Scott McDonald hit two for Motherwell and Celtic were beaten. The scenes at Easter Road were really quite astonishing as this news broke, confirming, against the odds, that Rangers were champions. The hope had turned to belief in what was a remarkable end to a remarkable season.

# SEASON 2004/05 QUIZ

How much can you still remember about last season?
Test your memory with some easy - and not so easy - questions!

**1** Who scored for Rangers on the opening day of the SPL campaign?

**2** How many new signings started the above game? Can you name them?

**3** Which ground attracted the biggest attendance on the last day of the SPL campaign?

**4** Rangers scored five goals in only one league clash last season. Who were the club's opponents that day?

**5** What was unique about Rangers' two goals in the 2-1 CIS Cup defeat of Celtic?

**6** How many points were dropped in the league games with Dundee United?

**7** Jean-Alain Boumsong scored once during his short stay in Glasgow. True or false?

**8** Rangers headed the SPL table for the first time last season after defeating which club?

**9** Who scored at Celtic Park in late February to famously end a five-year drought in the east end of Glasgow?

**10** Name the players who both scored twice at Ibrox in the last home game of the season.

Answers on page 62

# AND THE SCORER AGAINST CELTIC WAS ...

**Enter the surname of the scorer against Celtic in the appropriate boxes.**

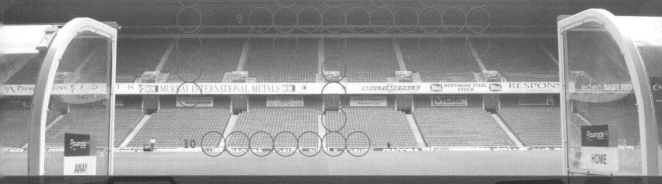

## ACROSS

**3** After crossing the great divide, this striker netted the winner in the Ibrox league clash of November 1989.

**7** This wee striker scored the only goal of the game when part three of Season 1998/99's treble was realised at Hampden in May.

**9** Club captain and legend, he scored the opener on final day in 1928 when Rangers' 25–year Scottish cup hoodoo came to an end.

**10** This player scored a hat-trick when Celtic provided the League Cup Final opposition in March 1984.

## DOWN

**1** Appearing as a substitute, this Scandinavian netted twice in the last seven minutes of the memorable New Year 1996/97 3–1 win at Ibrox.

**2** One of the great Old Firm goals was scored by this Englishman in September 1995 when Celtic lost in the league for the only time that season.

**4** His goal, from a free kick, was one of the memorable moments in the May final of 2002 Scottish Cup.

**5** In the first part of Season 2002/03's domestic treble, he scored the winner in the final of the CIS Cup.

**6** When Rangers secured the 1998/99 title at Celtic Park, his double on the day was crucial.

**8** This foreign star claimed the winner away to Celtic in March 1997, the last Old Firm clash before the nine–in–a–row was realised in May of the same year.

# Dado Prso, Bank of Scotland SPL Player of the Year for 2004/05, hit 21 goals last season. Do you remember all of these?

**1 LIVINGSTON (Home, 14.8.04)**
Rangers' first goal in their 2004/05 SPL journey came in the first five minutes of their first home game when Prso netted from close range with a shot under keeper McKenzie.

**2 HIBERNIAN (Home, 21.8.04)**
After setting up Arveladze for the opener, the hitman then claimed the second of the game with a perfect header across the keeper from Ricksen's deep delivery into the area.

**3 INVERNESS (Home, 19.9.04)**
His side's only goal of the ninety minutes was another header but this time Prso struck following Craig Moore's initial header from a Chris Burke corner.

**4 MOTHERWELL (Away, 17.10.04)**
Fresh from World Cup qualification duty, the big man's first of the day came at the end of a surging run when he lifted the ball over the outcoming Marshall.

**5 MOTHERWELL (Away, 17.10.04)**
Strong left-foot drive late-on, following excellent lead-up play by both Ricksen and Novo, sealed the points at a stage of the game when the home side were pushing hard for an equaliser.

**6 CELTIC (Home, 10.11.04)**
With only six minutes left in this Old Firm CIS Cup quarter-final tie at Ibrox, Prso coolly squared the game with a neat finish after Namouchi's drive was spilled by Marshall.

**7 HIBERNIAN (Away, 14.11.04)**
A penalty, superbly converted with his right foot, was the only goal of a fiery blue/green clash at Easter Road.

**8 CELTIC (Home, 20.11.04)**
In a crowded penalty area, his super header from Ricksen's delivery into the box was the goal that meant Rangers were two up before the interval.

**9 HIBERNIAN (Home, 12.2.05)**
His second of the day was a customarily emphatic left-foot drive from the edge of the area after taking a Novo pass on the run.

**10 KILMARNOCK (Home, 26.2.05)**
A prime candidate for goal of the season, this was an outstanding 25 yard right-foot shot that sailed over keeper Combe before dipping below the bar and into the net.

**11 ABERDEEN (Away, 1.5.05)**
His first of the game was arguably one of the season's finest goals. Following Novo's cutback from wide into the box, Prso conjured up a real piece of magic with a near-post back-heel that had class written all over it.

**12 ABERDEEN (Away, 1.5.05)**
For the second of his double that day, he produced another supreme example of the goalscoring art when, after controlling an Andrews header, he turned on a sixpence to blast home past Esson.

**T**he path to CIS cup glory was certainly not an easy one with the SPL power of Aberdeen, Celtic, Dundee United and Motherwell all determined to halt Rangers' progress at various stages of the competition.

Back in late September 2004, Alex McLeish's men travelled to Pittodrie to face an Aberdeen side unbeaten in seven games. That sequence was threatened, however, just before the interval when midfielder Fernando Ricksen opened the scoring with a stunning free-kick over the defensive wall that left keeper Preece with nothing but cold night air on his gloves. Steven Thompson made it two from close range late on in the second period (with Ricksen again involved) to ensure Aberdeen's first defeat of the season so far.

*Rangers: Klos, Khizanishvili, Boumsong, Moore, Vignal, Ricksen, Malcolm, Vanoli, Burke, Thompson and Arveladze.*

Rangers then played host to Celtic, in the knowledge, no doubt, that the last time they defeated Martin O'Neill's side was in the final of this very same competition back in March 2003. Although Hartson had given the visitors a second-half lead in this engrossing encounter, the Ibrox men equalised via substitute Dado Prso some six minutes before the end. The Croatian netted after Marshall failed to hold a Hamed Namouchi shot. Into extra-time, it was Shota Arveladze, another substitute, who claimed the winner with a magnificent left-foot drive following Ricksen's precision pass on the break. This superb strike meant that Celtic, for the first time in eight Old Firm clashes, were beaten and the celebrations could begin.

*Rangers: Klos, Khizanishvili, Boumsong, Andrews, Vignal, Ricksen, Rae, Namouchi, Lovenkrands, Thompson and Novo.*

**SEPTEMBER 2004 - ABERDEEN 0 RANGERS 2**

The following February, Dundee United provided semi-final opposition but there was little joy for the Tannadice outfit at the National Stadium that night. Early goals from Nacho Novo (springing the offside trap) and Prso (an angled header from fifteen yards) gave Rangers a double advantage prior to the half-time whistle. Novo even managed to miss a penalty for the first time in his career. Although Scotland pulled one back early in the next period and McIntyre subsequently hit the post, Rangers moved up a gear to put another five past Colgan for a rather satisfying seven. In order of play they came from Thomas Buffel (his first for the club), Ricksen (from a free-kick), Thompson (a brilliant volley), Novo (his 20th of the season) and Thompson again but this time from close range. Perhaps the biggest cheer of the evening, however, was reserved for the substitute appearance of homecoming hero Barry Ferguson, back from Blackburn.

***Rangers:*** *Waterreus, Ross, Andrews, Kyrgiakos, Ball, Ricksen, Vignal, Rae, Buffel, Novo and Prso.*

Much was expected of Terry Butcher's Motherwell before kick-off on cup final day but two goals adrift, in less than ten minutes, meant that their initial game plan required radical revision. Full-back Maurice Ross had opened the scoring with a delightful lift over the advancing Marshall before the head of Greek defender Sotirios Kyrgiakos made it two to the good. Partridge then replied for the Lanarkshire side but Ricksen kept distance between the teams with another super free kick and goal before the interval. It was all over as a contest

**FEBRUARY 2005 - RANGERS 7 DUNDEE UNITED 1**

when Novo lobbed Marshall at the start of the second forty-five but the actual scoring was not completed until late on when Kyrgiakos claimed his second with a powerful penalty box header from Ricksen's corner.

Rangers, who won the first ever League Cup tournament just after the Second World War in Season 1946/47, had now lifted this particular piece of silverware a record twenty-four times. For manager Alex McLeish, it was his sixth trophy in charge of the club.

*Rangers:* *Waterreus, Ross, Malcolm, Kyrgiakos, Ball, Ricksen, Vignal, Ferguson, Buffel, Novo and Prso.*

2005

THE CIS
INSURANCE CUP

CIS
Co-operative Insurance

**MARCH 2005 - RANGERS 5 MOTHERWELL 1**

# SO YOU THINK YOU KNOW RANGERS?

Test your Rangers knowledge with these questions from both the recent and not so recent history of the club.   Answers on page 62

**1** Rangers lifted the European Cup Winners' Cup in 1972 after defeating Moscow Dynamo 3-2 in the final. Who scored for the Light Blues that famous night?

**2** Rangers have been in two European finals. True or false?

**3** Name the 1930s item from the Trophy Room that is used before the first home match every New Year to toast the reigning monarch.

**4** What was the score in the final of the Centenary Scottish Cup in 1973?

**5** The attendance for a top of the table clash with Hibernian at Ibrox in April 1950 established a post-war British record for a league game. What was the approximate number of people in the crowd?

**6** He was one of the club's founders and Rangers' first-ever international player. Name him.

**7** The oil portrait of which legend takes pride of place above the splendid marble staircase inside the main entrance to Ibrox stadium?

**8** Who is the only man to have managed Rangers twice?

**9** Name the scorers on the last day of Season 2002/03 when Rangers defeated Dunfermline at Ibrox to lift the title.

**10** He always carried a champagne cork in his pocket for luck. Who was this legendary captain of Rangers?

# SPOT THE DIFFERENCE

Can you spot the eight differences between these two Broxi Bear photos?

Answers on page 62

# SPOT THE BALL

Can you spot where the ball should be?

Answer on page 62

# RANGERS
## FOOTBALL CLUB

# MR STRUTH

The Ibrox Trophy Room, with its spectacular display of silverware, porcelain, crystal and memorabilia stretching back to the very foundations of the club, was opened in 1959 when Scot Symon was manager of Rangers. Amongst all these wonderful treasures, displayed in a suitably prominent position on the wall at the back of the room, is an oil painting surrounded by miniature replicas of many decades of League Championship flags. The oil painting is of none other than the legendary William Struth - the greatest-ever manager of Rangers.

Bill Struth was a stonemason by trade and, as a young man, competed for cash by running at athletic meetings throughout the country. He was appointed trainer of Clyde in 1908 (at the age of 33) and arrived at Ibrox in 1914 to fill the same role with Rangers. Following the death of club secretary-manager William Wilton in a 1920 boating accident, Struth was appointed manager of the club ... and a legend was born.

His astonishing record of success speaks for itself - in an amazing 34 years at the helm, Rangers lifted the League Championship 18 times, the Scottish Cup 10 times, the League Cup twice, the Glasgow Cup 18 times and the Glasgow Charity Cup 20 times. In Season 1929/30, the club won every competition that they were eligible to enter. This record haul comprised the League Championship, the Scottish Cup, the Glasgow Cup, the Glasgow Charity Cup, the Reserve League Championship and the Reserve Cup! As he once famously said 'Let the others come after us. We welcome the chase'.

Following the introduction of the League Cup for Season 1946/47 (Rangers lifted the trophy that first year of competition) his side became the first Scottish team to secure the domestic treble in 1948/49 – two years later. Additionally, in the first 18 years of his Ibrox management, Rangers won the league title 14 times, finishing second in three out of the four other years and third in the remaining year.

He became a director of Rangers in 1947 and, seven years later in the summer of 1954, retired as manager. Aged 81, the great man passed away in September 1956 making 2006, the 50th anniversary of his death.

Needless to say, his memory lives on forever.

scored! Earlier in the campaign he had conceded only one goal in the month of September and just two the following month October.

### Ronald Waterreus

Signed as a replacement for the injured Stefan Klos, Dutchman Ronald Waterreus achieved heroic status in just his third game with Rangers when, in the crucial east end of Glasgow Old Firm clash in February, he defied the Celtic attack time after time to keep the Light Blues in the game during a torrid first forty-five minutes. 34-year-old Waterrreus, a close friend of Arthur

### Stefan Klos

Stefan Klos was at his usual consistent best for all of his 34 consecutive appearances in the first half of last season before sustaining a cruciate ligament injury in January 2005. This freak training accident (he caught his studs on the Murray Park turf) meant that he missed the remainder of the campaign. Since arriving from Germany in December 1998, the goalkeeper (a Champions League winner with Borussia Dortmund) hardly missed a game in that six year period with Rangers until that fateful winter's day. Now contracted to the club until 2007, the fans have not forgotten the 2005 New Year's Day joust at Tannadice last season when his mere presence in the opposition box for a corner caused such panic in the last minute of the game that Hamed Namouchi

Numan, spent some ten years with PSV Eindhoven (winning four championships in his homeland during that time) before deciding to join Manchester City in the Premiership for Season 2004/05 as deputy to first choice England man David James. At Euro 2004 in Portugal he was the No 2 goalkeeper in Dick Advocaat's Holland side. After his first outing for the Light Blues in the early February CIS Cup semi-final against Dundee United at Hampden, Waterrreus, apart from one game, was an ever-present up to and including the end of season clash with Hibernian at Easter Road.

**Alan Hutton**
The young full-back, under contract until year 2007, made his first appearance last season when Rangers lost 1-0 at Celtic Park in late August. His next game was the 4-1 away win over Livingston at Almondvale in November before making the first of four consecutive starts, in December and January, beginning with the SPL away victory at Kilmarnock the week before Christmas. Then, after performing really well in the home and away triumphs over Hibernian (3-0) and Celtic (2-0) respectively, Hutton tragically broke his right leg during the late February meeting with Kilmarnock at Ibrox, ruling him out

of the remainder of last season's title race. On the night of Sunday 22 March, it was good to see him - albeit in suit and tie - on the Ibrox turf with the rest of the squad as they celebrated a famous title win.

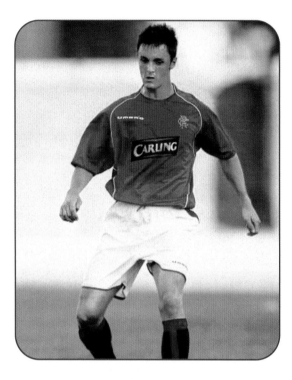

## Maurice Ross

One of the best quotes of Season 2004/05 was surely from Maurice Ross describing his reaction to scoring the opener on CIS Cup final day at Hampden - 'I was just screaming like a lassie.' The defender made 18 starting appearances last term with the obvious highlight being that day at the National Stadium in March when he not only scored his only goal of the entire campaign (a striker's assured finish for Rangers' first of five) but also hardly put a foot wrong with a near faultless defensive display. In Rangers' penultimate away game at Pittodrie, Ross filled the left back position as both Michael Ball and Gregory Vignal were injured and did not look out of place at all.

## Michael Ball

When Michael Ball arrived at Rangers from Everton in 2001, at £6.5m, he was Scotland's most expensive player but serious injury and then contract problems meant that, by early February, he had only made a total of 61 appearances for the Ibrox club. By the March/April latter stages of the season, however, the steely Ball was back as a regular in the side, impressing the fans again with the cool authority of a fine, fine footballer. It should not be forgotten that he was a regular man-of-the-match winner in Everton games with the likes of Liverpool and Manchester United down south and was picked for England in Sven-Goran Erikson's first game in charge of the national side.

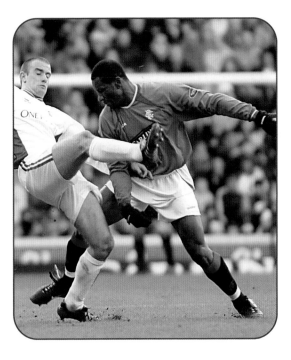

## Marvin Andrews

Prior to the start of the 2004/05 campaign, most observers felt that Marvin Andrews, newly signed from Livingston, would not be an automatic first team choice but more of a squad player in the coming months. At that time, few would surely have anticipated the huge effect that the big man had on Rangers, the Ibrox masses and the Scottish game in general by the summer of 2005. His first outing was in the 4-0 home win over Livingston in August with his first goal for the club coming in early October when Kilmarnock lost 2-0 at Ibrox. Partnering Boumsong in defence, he was quite superb and, indeed, nearly hit a hat-trick in a man-of-the-match display. A devout Christian, Andrews was then an ever-present in the side (partnering Boumsong, Khizanishvili, Malcolm or Kyrgiakos in central defence) before sustaining cruciate ligament damage in the Dens Park clash with Dundee in mid-March after putting Rangers ahead late-on in the game with a vital header. Declining to go under the knife and have an operation, big Marv decided to place his faith in God instead and subsequently astounded everybody by appearing, less than six weeks later, in the starting line-up for the last Old Firm game of the season. He then featured in all the remaining fixtures, with the added bonus of a goal in the penultimate home game against Hearts (2-1, 7.5.05). In the eyes of the Rangers fans, he was, quite simply, a candidate for player of the year.

## Bob Malcolm

Equally at home in either defence or midfield, the versatile Bob Malcolm's first appearance in blue last season

### Zurab Khizanishvili

The cultured Georgian, who rarely looks uncomfortable on the ball, started 22 domestic and European games throughout the 2004/05 period, filling both the right back and central defensive positions for the club. Now in his third season at Ibrox (he joined from Dundee in the summer of 2003), Khizanishvili is a footballer in the true sense of the word - someone who makes the beautiful game actually seem that way and is a joy to watch on the field of play.

### Ian Murray

With his Hibernian contract expired, the 24-year-old, former captain of the club signed a three-year Rangers deal in early June, joining the ranks of players such as Andy Goram and Kenny Miller who previously arrived

was for the CIS Cup tie at Pittodrie when Aberdeen were ousted from the competition on the back of a 2-0 defeat. In total, he started 22 games and, although only claiming one goal in all these outings, Malcolm ensured that it was of the special variety. Visitors Dundee, pre-Christmas 2004, started the second half of this SPL match two goals behind after Novo and Prso had established an early lead for Rangers. Within less than five minutes of the game recommencing, Malcolm hit a glorious left-foot drive from the edge of the box that soared into the net past the reach of Soutar. It was a magnificent strike and a magical moment quite appropriate for that yuletide time of the year. It certainly brought the crowd to their feet on a cold winter's afternoon in Govan.

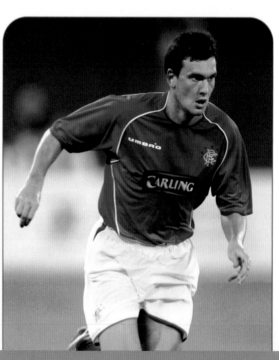

at Ibrox from Easter Road. Murray, a real competitor, is extremely comfortable on either foot and can play in a variety of positions (including left full-back, midfield or central defence) with equal success. As manager of Hibernian, it was Alex McLeish who actually spotted his potential at an early age and signed him when he was just a teenager of 16. Some two years later, after making his first-team debut at 18, Murray secured a permanent place in the Hibernian squad. Following the completion of his Bosman move west, he said: 'Of course, it's a massive step up for me because there are different pressures at Rangers but I feel that I'm ready to step into that environment. Rangers are a massive club and, when I found out they were interested, I didn't hesitate.'

### Brahim Hemdani
Born in Colombes, France, of Algerian parents, 27-year-old Brahim Hemdani joined Marseilles in 2001 (after a £2 million transfer from Strasbourg) and was captain of the side that reached the Gothenburg final of the UEFA Cup two seasons ago. However, because of a contract dispute, the experienced campaigner only made eleven appearances (with four of them as substitute) for Philippe Trousier's team in 2004/05. Strong and versatile, he is equally at home right or left midfield but probably his best position is a holding role just in front

of the defence. Alex McLeish had been tracking the player for some time and was naturally delighted to have secured his Bosman signature on a four-year-deal in the summer of 2005.

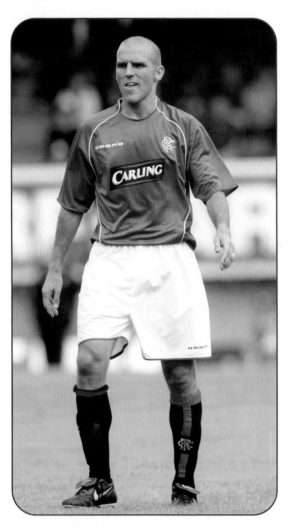

club, Rae's solitary goal of last season was probably, in his eyes, a candidate for Goal of the Season! It was the third of the day's trio against Dunfermline in mid-January and was a strong downward header to beat the Pars keeper. His contribution, especially during the latter part of the league race, was immense, with his Premiership experience of huge importance as Rangers kept up the challenge until the final whistle of the final game.

### Hamed Namouchi
Now in his third season after arriving in the summer of 2003, French-Tunisian Hamed Namouchi was on the score sheet in only his second start of the domestic programme. Following his 2004/05 debut in the 5-0 thrashing of Aberdeen (31.10.04), the talented youngster netted in the next outing when Rangers travelled to West Lothian to record a 4-1 win

### Alex Rae
After joining the club from Wolves for the start of the 2004/05 period, true Rangers man Alex Rae tore a calf muscle at the very beginning of the late August Celtic Park fixture, just four games into the new SPL campaign. The tough-tackling midfielder was then out of action for several weeks before returning to the fray in the CIS Cup victory over the same Celtic opponents at Ibrox in November. As a supporter of the

starting line-up for most of September and October, injury continued to be an uninvited house guest. Fit again by the latter part of the programme, it was obviously difficult for him to break into a winning team but the fans' favourite will naturally be ready when the call comes from Alex McLeish in 2005/06.

### Jose Karl Pierre Fanfan

The 6ft 2in defender and former captain of Paris St Germain was another of Alex McLeish's summer 2005 signings. Strong, superb in the air and extremely comfortable with the ball at his feet, the 30-year-old (who is of Guadaloupean descent) joined Rangers on a three year contract after having won every major domestic trophy in France. Last

over Livingston. A fine finish from a Vignal ball, it was the last goal of the Sunday afternoon television game. Later that same month, but this time on European duty, Namouchi claimed another - after good play down the right by Novo - in the UEFA Cup tie with Grazer AK. That 3-0 victory, incidentally, had taken Rangers to the top of Group F in the competition.

### Chris Burke

Period 2004/05 was a disappointing season for the young Glaswegian who missed a fair chunk of the campaign through injury. Indeed, right at the start of the second half on the first day at Pittodrie in early August, he was carried-off the field suffering the effects of a virus problem. Although he was in the

season, he was part of the PSG team that drew 0-0 at Stamford Bridge against Chelsea in the Champions League. Before his time in the French capital, he played for Monaco and, prior to that, made his name at Lens where his teammates included El Hadji-Diouf (now with Bolton in the Premiership) and Olivier Dacourt of Roma. A close friend of Dado Prso from their time together at Monaco, the imposing stopper arrived at Ibrox for no fee because of a release clause in his PSG contract.

**Nacho Novo**
With his blistering pace used to great effect, both through the middle and out wide, Nacho Novo's first season in the blue of Rangers was a huge success. From a scoring point of view, his most important goal was on championship day in Edinburgh when his strike was all that separated the sides at Easter Road. Earlier, before the turn of the year, the Spaniard hit doubles in the SPL clashes with Dundee (2-0, 26.9.04), Aberdeen (5-0, 31.10.04), Hearts (3-2, 28.11.04) and Motherwell (4-1, 27.12.04) and then scored another brace at Hampden in February when Dundee United were demolished 7-1 in the semi-final of the CIS Cup. Although the goals dried up somewhat in the latter stages of league run-in - he still ended the campaign as top scorer on 25 remember - his overall contribution to the team remained exceptional, despite the fact that hernia problems meant that he was far from 100% fit. At that time, his wide-right role was another weapon in Rangers' armoury.

### Peter Lovenkrands

The Dane was another player whose 2004/05 season was dramatically curtailed by injury. Early on in that period, in the third league game, Lovenkrands netted number four in the 4-1 home win over Hibernian. Then, exactly two months later on a UEFA Cup night, the winger scored the opener in one of Rangers' finest European displays for some time when McLeish's side crushed Amica Wronki 5-0 away in Poland. His remaining goals last season came in consecutive championship fixtures - the 5-0 beating of Aberdeen and the 4-1 triumph over Livingston in October and November 2004 respectively.

### Steven Thompson

Seven of the ten goals that Steven Thompson netted last season all came after he appeared as a substitute in various games, including the European clashes with CSKA Moscow (1-1, 25.8.04) and Amica Wronki (5-0, 21.10.04). Another two of the seven came in the CIS Cup semi-final at Hampden when, despite his late appearance with just fifteen minutes to go, Thompson hit a memorable double in the tie with his old club Dundee United - 7-1, final score. Prior to this, his season had been severely interrupted and torn ankle ligaments meant several weeks out of action. By the time he was fully fit again, Prso and Novo were firing on all cylinders and a place on the bench, therefore, continued for the latter stages of the title run-in.

# WHO SAID THAT LAST SEASON?

Answers on page 62

1 "For me, it doesn't matter whether the pitch is grass or plastic. By complaining, it is only making excuses and I don't want that."

2 "I'm still a Rangers supporter, I follow every single game and I hope we are going to win the title. If that happens, then it would make me a champion and I'd feel like one as well because I played half a season."

3 "One minute you're the brightest star since the one over Bethlehem, the next it's all taken away from you."

4 "I was just screaming like lassie. I was delighted to get a goal because it's rare for me."

5 "A player of my ability is not a Ronaldo or a Zidane. I am a player that needs to work hard for myself and the team and to get recognition like that is fantastic."

6 "You only spoke when spoken to by the first team back then. I remember Ted McMinn would ask me if his boots were done and, if I said: "Do them yourself", I'd get locked in the laundry cupboard for 40 minutes until I apologised. That was part of your education."

7 "You can only do so much. If people don't realise what we've got to do, then there's no use them pulling the jersey on."

8 "I saw Real Madrid's Luis Figo being hit by a pig's head a couple of years ago after he joined them from Barcelona. I suppose anything can happen at a football match these days."

9 "He was always crazy about Rangers. He was impressed by the club when we faced PSV Eindhoven in the Champions League and he is a very close friend of Arthur Numan."

10 "This is part of my family - from the kit man, Jimmy Bell, to the tea lady. I have missed everybody since I went away."

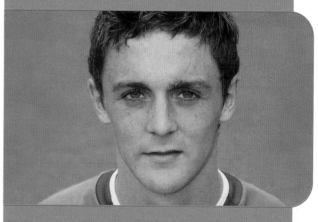

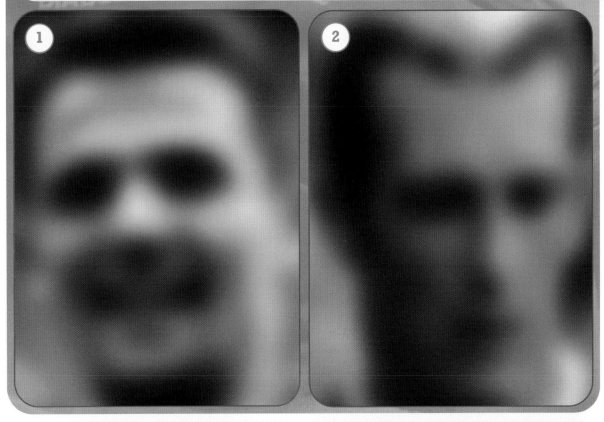

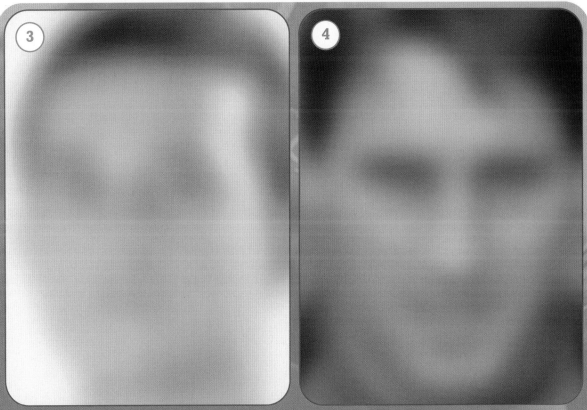

**Nacho Novo ended his first season at Ibrox as top scorer with a total of 25 goals to his name. Here's a reminder of just twelve of them:**

**1 CSKA MOSCOW (Away, 10.8.04)**
The wee man's first-ever competitive Rangers goal was in this Champions League qualifier when he slammed home after Dado Prso's initial effort had been blocked by the keeper.

**2 DUNDEE (Away, 26.9.04)**
After appearing as a second half substitute in this SPL clash with his former club (the game was still finely balanced at 0-0), Novo claimed his first Rangers league goal after a Chris Burke nod across the penalty area set him up to score with his left from close-in.

**3 DUNDEE UTD (Home, 24.10.04)**
Deadly and accurate, this 20-yard drive, 20 minutes before the end, left keeper Jarvis without a prayer in a game Novo only started because Peter Lovenkrands fell sick just before kick-off.

**4 LIVINGSTON (Away, 7.11.04)**
Fernando Ricksen's cross to the back post was volleyed home in quite emphatic style for Rangers' second of the game.

**5 CELTIC (Home, 20.11.04)**
Following a reckless lunge by Valgaeren, Novo's record of never having missed a penalty continued when he converted his third spot kick of the campaign.

**6 HEARTS (Home, 28.11.04)**
Racing on to a Khizanishvili pass, Gordon was well beaten when the wee man showed superb composure by lifting the ball over the Hearts keeper.

**7 HEARTS (Home, 28.11.04)**
Hamed Namouchi's flighted ball was headed home from close range to put Rangers top of the league following this 3-2 victory.

**8 MOTHERWELL (Home, 27.12.04)**
After running on to Arveladze's delightful through-ball in fifteen minutes, the Spaniard clinically buried past Corr for his 17th of the season.

**9 DUNDEE UTD (Hampden, 2.2.05)**
For the crucial opener in the CIS Cup semi-final, he brilliantly sprang the offside trap before rounding keeper Colgan to net from Thomas Buffel's incisive ball.

**10 CELTIC (Away, 20.2.05)**
A superb lob over the advancing Douglas was the icing on the cake as the Light Blues won at Celtic Park for the first time in five years. For many Rangers fans, this was the goal of the season.

**11 HEARTS (Away, 2.3.05)**
Dado Prso's pinpoint pass enabled him to race away and slot decisively past Scotland man Gordon.

**12 HIBERNIAN (Away, 22.5.05)**
His first goal in two months, a powerful low drive across the Hibernian keeper in the second half of the season's last game, was absolutely crucial on the day that the SPL Championship returned to Ibrox.

# THE MAN IN CHARGE

At Scotland's National Stadium, on Sunday March 29, 2005, Alex McLeish celebrated his sixth trophy as manager of Rangers after his side had comprehensively demolished Motherwell 5-1 in the final of the CIS Insurance Cup. Since his arrival at the club in December 2001 until the end of Season 2004/05, McLeish had now brought two SPL Championships, two Scottish Cups and three CIS (League) Cups back to the Ibrox Trophy Room.

That late March day was indeed a sweet occasion for the manager (his first silverware in some twenty-two months) who had been the subject of a huge amount of unnecessary criticism earlier in the campaign when many were calling for his dismissal. Following the Hampden triumph he was quoted as saying: 'Other people might have walked away but that's not my style. I was confident in the support I had from my chairman and the chief executive Martin Bain. A lot of the criticism I had to endure was disrespectful but that's the idiosyncrasies of the way some people work.

'I knew there was going to be a bit of pain last season. When you see the fall-out of the players that we lost without the funds to replace them, it was always going to be tough. A lot of people didn't appreciate that.

'I could have walked away after the treble season and said that I saw the writing on the wall here, but that's not my style ... I knew that if we could be a wee bit patient and persevere, we could be a real threat to Celtic again. We still have a wee bit to go because we are a young and inexperienced team.'

One of the many Hampden highlights for all friends of Rangers that March afternoon was the look of real satisfaction on the face of Alex McLeish following the final whistle celebrations. Of course, that look was back again at Easter Road in May when his team dramatically reclaimed the league title. It is worth remembering that, in head-to-head encounters when Martin O'Neill was Celtic manager, Alex McLeish won more silverware than his former Old Firm opposite number in the same period.

**Here's to you, Big Eck!**

# ALEX'S TEAM TALK

Answers on page 62

Manager Alex McLeish obviously speaks about his team a great deal but which of his players was he talking about when he said the following last season:

**1** 'His work rate has been outstanding. When we went to Motherwell a few weeks ago, we went three goals up but they pulled us back to 3-2. Towards the end, they were trying to launch balls into the box and he ran 30 yards to close down his opponent. He conceded a throw-in after which the referee blew for full-time. Had he not shown the desire to get there, then who knows what might have happened.'

**2** 'I said to him this morning that we all see him as Superman; he doesn't get injuries. When he does, he makes sure it's a good one.'

**3** 'His use of the ball from the back was excellent and his reaction to the second ball for his goal was tremendous.'

**4** 'He was playing through what to other people would have been a serious injury. He's suffering with a groin problem and that can be painful. But that's the kind of man he is, he just shrugs pain off.'

**5** 'He is great for the dressing room and he is a great figure for the fans. We all know that he gives 100% and he brings technique to the team as well.'

**6** 'Henrik Larsson arrived in Scotland having played a similar role at Feyenoord. He is an international player and we hope his Rangers career sees him win many more caps for his country. He has got the capabilities to do well here.'

**7** 'He is a great footballer and he is probably a guy who wants to make up for lost time. I was amazed that nobody took the chance on him from the Premiership because he is a player I believe will excel in the next few years.'

**8** 'He looked assured and very positive. I think he's a player who can get a good relationship with the Rangers fans.'

**9** 'His performances just get better and he's not just in there breaking things up. He's becoming a key player for Rangers. He's a good passer of the ball. I am not saying he's going to open doors like the Zidanes or the Tottis, but what he does do is play to his strengths.'

**10** 'He had eight stitches inserted in a head wound and he looks like Frankenstein in the dressing room - appropriate for Hallowe'en, I suppose.'

A CHANGED MAN

# FERNANDO RICKSEN

A dynamic, driving force in midfield, the tireless Fernando Ricksen was voted Rangers Player of the Year last season as well as being named joint winner of the Scottish Players' Player of the Year award with John Hartson. The Dutchman, now contracted until 2009, never missed a single game in the 2004/05 period and was a model of consistency, from August start until May finish – throughout the whole campaign. There can be little doubt that the fans were now seeing a different Ricksen from the player who had previously missed 18 club games through suspension and was rarely out of the headlines.

Although Ricksen started the first few games of the 2004/05 period at full-back, by the end of August circumstances dictated that Alex McLeish would move him forwards to midfield. His first goal came north, at Pittodrie, in the CIS Cup tie with Aberdeen (2-0, 22.9.04) and was a quite wonderful free-kick over the red wall that zoomed into the net. Interestingly, the Dutchman's third conversion of the campaign was another thunderous shot in another clash with the team from the Granite City - on this occasion, however, it was not a deadball situation but a 25 yard blast from a partial clearance after Steven Thompson had come close in the dying minutes of what eventually turned out to be a 5-0 October demolition of Aberdeen.

Fernando Ricksen, who spent three hours a day in the gym during the summer of 2004 before returning for pre-season training, claimed nine goals in total last term with six of them coming after the turn of the year. During that time, he netted in league victories over Livingston (home, 3-0) and Dundee (away, 2-0) as well as scoring the late, late winner from the spot at Tynecastle in a rather controversial 2-1 March win. Despite the huge pressure of the moment, that penalty was despatched past Gordon in goal with real authority.

Additionally, his name was on the Hampden score sheet in both the semi-final and final of the CIS Cup competition (7-1 v Dundee United and 5-1 v Motherwell respectively) and, as captain in place of the injured Stefan Klos, led his team up the steps of the main stand to lift the trophy on that memorable March afternoon at the National Stadium. Of course, it was not the first time in his career that the player had worn a captain's armband - he was captain of the Dutch under-23 side during his time in Holland with AZ Alkmaar.

There is no doubt that the changed Fernando Ricksen was a revelation in the blue of Rangers last season, proving the point that changes certainly are for the better.

# BELGIAN BLUE

# THOMAS BUFFEL

## Little known in Scotland before his January 2005 arrival, this player was making headlines by the following May.

Under new coach Ruud Gullit, Thomas Buffel was far from enjoying the best of times at Dutch club Feyenoord (he hardly played in six months) before signing a four-and-a-half year contract with Rangers in January 2005. Prior to Gullit's arrival at the club where the player had spent both his youth and formative years, the young Belgian was something of a revelation, playing as a second striker just behind main man (and ex-Celt) Pierre van Hooijdonk. Without a doubt, his scoring record of 32 goals in two seasons during that period speaks for itself.

Buffel's first start for his new club was in the 3-0 home victory over Dunfermline in mid-January, before he claimed his first Rangers goal, some two weeks later, in the 7-1 CIS Cup demolition of Dundee United at Hampden. With his best display to date in the blue, the player set up Nacho Novo for the important opener and then scored Rangers' third of the game at a stage when it looked as if a second half Dundee United revival was on the cards. The following week, he netted again in the Ibrox clash with high-flying UEFA Cup hopefuls Hibernian (3-0, 12.2.05) after unveiling an impressive change of pace in a counter-attack involving both Novo and Prso.

Fast forward to early May with a match fit Buffel (only 24 years of age remember) now playing in his favoured position just behind the striker, in this case Prso, and now beginning to justify the £3.2m price tag. In the penultimate home game of the season (a 2-1 win over Hearts), the Belgian scored with a header, supplied Marvin Andrews for the second and also hit the underside of the bar with a magnificent 16-yard side-foot shot in the second half of the game. A man-of-the-match display for sure. He was just as impressive seven days later but this time his goal tally was two when Motherwell were beaten 4-1. His brace that sunny afternoon in Govan were both excellent finishes: firstly after speeding away from his marker to bury past Marshall and secondly after hitting a solid penalty box drive past the keeper.

After the win over Hearts, Belgian coach Aime Antheunis was quoted as saying: 'When Thomas plays behind the main striker, he can score goals, he can create goals and he can supply passes to runners from midfield. He is so good at holding the ball and feeding other players. He has the vision to fill that free role and I am sure Rangers will get most out of him there.'

The feeling remains that Thomas Buffel is going to be an important Rangers player for many years to come.

# 51 AND COUNTING

**W**hen Rangers dramatically won the Scottish Premier League at the end of Season 2004/05, it was Championship number fifty-one for the club. With plenty of interesting and unusual facts and figures, here is a very brief history of that magical half-hundred plus one:

**1890/91:** Rangers shared the first-ever Scottish Football League championship with Dumbarton (following a 2-2 play-off draw) after both teams had ended the actual campaign on 29 points.

**1898/99:** Winning every league game, Hibernian were 10-0 casualties along the way. Schoolmaster RC Hamilton hit 21 goals in the 18 league encounters.

**1899/1900:** The title was taken seven points ahead of Celtic.

**1900/01:** Three-in-a-row with their Old Firm rivals again second but this time six points adrift.

**1901/02:** To win the championship, Celtic required five points from five games at one stage but a 4-2 January victory at Parkhead turned the tide for Rangers.

**1910/11:** With the league campaign now 34 games, Celtic's six year domination was brought to an end. Centre-forward Willie Reid hit 38 goals in 33 appearances.

**1911/12:** The championship was won by six points from Celtic. During this season, because of a national coal strike, Rangers actually supplied the fuel for a train to take them to Kirkcaldy for a match with Raith Rovers!

**1912/13:** Four points behind Celtic with 14 games to play, the Light Blues went on an unbeaten run to take the title.

**1917/18:** Before the final game, both halves of the Old Firm had 54 points. Rangers then beat Clyde 2-1 but Celtic only managed a 1-1 draw at home to Motherwell.

**1919/20:** 71 points from a marathon 42 game season and, for the first time, over a century of goals - 106 to be precise.

**1920/21:** With legend Bill Struth now in charge, the opening 23 games realised 44 points out of a possible 46. Celtic's Ibrox win in January was to be their last in this corresponding fixture for 62 years!

**1922/23:** In the season that Dane Carl Hansen became the first foreign player to net in an Old Firm clash (Rangers won 2-0 at Ibrox in January), the Light Blues finished five points ahead of Airdrie.

**1923/24:** Unbeaten until the 2-1 reversal away to Ayr in January, centre-forward Geordie Henderson was top

scorer (with 23 goals this time) for the second successive season.

**1924/25:** It was Airdrie, for the third year in a row, pushing Rangers the hardest and, with one game to go, they sat just one point behind. Henderson's strike rate was an even more impressive 27 league goals.

**1926/27:** Number 15 of 50 and Bob McPhail (230 Rangers career league goals) arrived from Airdrie to form an outstanding left-wing partnership with the 'wee blue devil' Alan Morton.

**1927/28:** 24 goals in the first six games and the team were on the way to equalling Celtic's record of 16 flags. Jimmy Fleming - 33 goals in 34 games.

**1928/29:** Fleming hit 33 in 35

appearances in the season the new 10,000 seat Grandstand was opened.

**1929/30:** Bill Struth's team won every tournament available to them – the League Championship, the Scottish Cup, the Glasgow Cup and the Charity Cup.

**1930/31:** A club record of five successive titles. Victory against Celtic in the Ne'erday clash set Struth's side off on an unbeaten twelve game run.

**1932/33:** Motherwell (first, third and second in the previous three campaigns) were again formidable but Rangers' 3-1 Fir Park win in February was crucial.

**1933/34:** With 20 goals in the first four games, Rangers would end their title defence with 118 in total. Jimmy

Smith (41 from 32 appearances) claimed 12 of that initial 20 back at the start.

**1934/35:** In the first match, Smith hit six as Dunfermline suffered a 7-1 thrashing. Celtic's challenge was strong but a crowd of 83,000 viewed their 2-1 Ibrox January defeat as the beginning of the end. Incidentally, when Kilmarnock won 3-2 in Glasgow in December, it was Rangers' first home league defeat in three years!

**1936/37:** Aberdeen were the main challengers but, right from the word go,

Rangers were consistent with a run of 17 games without a loss. Jerry Dawson, the prince of goalkeepers, was an ever-present in the team.

**1938/39:** Despite losing 6-2 to Celtic early-on, their rivals in green were still left 11 points in the distance when the trophy was being awarded to Rangers. Centre-forward Willie Thornton had now been joined by two other legends bearing the same Christian name - Waddell and Woodburn - in the last season before the outbreak of the Second World War.

**1946/47:** For the first post-war campaign, Hibernian became a force in the east and ended the period just two points adrift. Top scorers for Rangers were Jimmy Duncanson and Willie Thornton with 18 league goals each.

**1948/49:** On the last day of the title race, leaders Dundee required one point at Falkirk to become champions. They lost and Rangers 4-1 triumph away to Albion Rovers (a Thornton hat-trick) ensured number 26 of 50. The Ibrox men also became the first Scottish side to lift the domestic treble of League Championship, Scottish Cup and League Cup in one season.

**1949/50:** After drawing 0-0 with second placed Hibernian in the penultimate game, Rangers needed just one point from their last match - a 2-2 draw away to Third Lanark guaranteed just that. Of the famed 'Iron Curtain' defence, four members (Brown, Young, Cox and McColl) never missed a league clash all season. Additionally, Shaw and Woodburn missed only one each.

**1952/53:** This year's title was won on goal difference from Hibernian after

Willie Waddell's late equaliser against Queen of the South at Palmerston Park ensured a 1-1 draw in the final campaign outing.

**1955/56:** Despite winning only one of their opening six league encounters, a 23 match unbeaten run meant celebrations in due course. Queen of the South lost 8-0 at Ibrox in the very first Scottish fixture to be played under floodlights.

**1956/57:** Although Hearts led for most of the journey, 11 wins and a draw in the remaining 12 games (including a vital 1-0 Tynecastle victory) meant that Rangers crossed the finishing line two points ahead of the Edinburgh side. Centre-forward Max Murray hit 29 goals, almost a third of the team's 96 total.

**1958/59:** Going into the final ninety minutes, Hearts were again close and only two points behind. Amazingly, relegation threatened Aberdeen won 2-1 at Ibrox but Hearts also lost - at Celtic Park! The title was back for the third time in four seasons.

**1960/61:** The championship was won on the last day of the season (by one point from Kilmarnock) when a 7-3 victory over their Ayrshire rivals Ayr United grabbed the headlines. In the second game of that campaign, Celtic were crushed 5-1 in the east end of Glasgow.

**1962/63:** This was the year of the big freeze and Rangers, after beating Celtic 4-0 on New Year's Day, did not play another game until 9 March. A truly great team had now emerged - Ritchie, Shearer, Caldow, Greig, McKinnon, Baxter, Henderson, McMillan, Millar, Brand and Wilson.

**1963/64:** Old friends Celtic were beaten five times in five games and the period ended with the first domestic treble in fifteen years. It was the third championship in four years, the fourth in six years and the sixth in nine years.

**1974/75:** Jock Wallace's side finally ended nine years of Celtic domination when Colin Stein's goal in the 1-1 draw with Hibernian meant not only a share of the points but also the league title. Of the 38,585 at Easter road that day, over 30,000 were believed to be Rangers fans!

**1975/76:** Unbeaten in the new (10 team) Premier League from early December until the end of the campaign, Derek Johnstone claimed the winner at Tannadice on title day. Another season of triple glory - the third in the club's history.

**1977/78:** In the opening Old Firm clash, Rangers were 2-0 down at half-time but a second forty-five revival (including two goals from Gordon Smith and one from Johnstone) secured a famous victory. A fourth domestic treble was also realised.

**1986/87:** The arrival of Graeme Souness (and subsequent signings of Englishmen Terry Butcher, Chris Woods and Graham Roberts) certainly transformed the club, with Butcher's headed goal at Pittodrie in early May the reason for some serious celebrations. At one stage in the league, Rangers were nine points behind Celtic.

**1988/89:** Champion status (the first of nine-in-a-row) was confirmed on the day that Hearts were beaten 4-0 at Ibrox with top scorer for the season Kevin Drinkell claiming a brace.

**1989/90:** The year of Maurice Johnston, in more ways than one. Although Trevor Steven netted the title-winning goal at Tannadice in April, ex-Celt 'Mo' was top scorer with 15. The Light Blues' January Old Firm win was the first in a Celtic Park New Year derby for more than 20 years.

**1990/91:** For the third season in a row, Aberdeen were the closest challengers but this time around the

team from the north required only one point at Ibrox on the last day of the season to claim the crown. With Walter Smith now in charge, Mark Hateley's two famous goals in that game made him an instant legend.

**1991/92:** 'Golden Boot' winner Ally McCoist hit 34 of the record 101 goal total and the team won 19 of their 22 away league fixtures.

**1992/93:** From late August until late March, the fans saw 29 games come and go without defeat. Add another 34 McCoist goals to the mix and five-in-a-row was in the bag. Oh yes, there was also the small matter of the club's fifth domestic treble to consider!

**1993/94:** Mark Hateley, top scorer with 22 league goals, netted at Parkhead in January (Rangers were three up in less than half an hour) and became the first Englishman to win the Football Writers' Player of the Year award. Celtic ended their own league journey without a top three place.

**1994/95:** This was the year that the hugely talented Dane Brian Laudrup became the pin-up of the Ibrox masses. Surprisingly, Motherwell took second spot (albeit 15 points adrift) with Celtic again nowhere to be seen.

**1995/96:** With their Old Firm rivals back in the hunt, wayward genius Paul Gascoigne hit a hat-trick against Aberdeen in the game that eventually decided the trophy's destination. The previous September, he had scored a magnificent goal in the east end of Glasgow on the day that Celtic suffered their only defeat of the entire league campaign.

**1996/97:** Nine-in-a-row was eventually realised at Tannadice when Laudrup's rare headed strike (the only goal of the game) ensured full points against Dundee United. Truthfully, the Dane had been sensational all season.

**1998/99:** In over 100 years of Scottish League football, no Rangers team had ever won the championship at the home of their greatest rivals but a 3-0 triumph at Celtic Park on a Sunday in May changed all that. Lorenzo Amoruso became the first foreign player to skipper Rangers to the title in the year that treble number six was registered.

**1999/2000:** 21 points ahead of Celtic by the end, this season included comprehensive away victories over Aberdeen (5-1), Motherwell (5-1) and Dundee (7-1) as well as excellent 4-2 and 4-0 Old Firm wins.

**2002/03:** The closest league race for many years was only decided on the last day of the season when Rangers' 6-1 defeat of Dunfermline at Ibrox edged out Celtic on goal difference. Barry Ferguson was immense and fully deserved the honour of lifting the other two domestic trophies for the seventh treble in the club's history.

**2004/05:** Another last day of the season nail-biter. Early on, after just five games, Rangers were seven points behind leaders Celtic but McLeish's men kept believing right 'til the end and reaped the reward. They all played their part but special mention surely to Marvin Andrews, a giant of a man in more ways than one.

# Without a doubt, the signing of the season!

On the final day of the first month of 2005, right at the end of the transfer window period, there was a worrying time for all friends of Rangers Football Club when it looked as if Barry Ferguson's proposed return to the club from Blackburn Rovers might not actually happen after all. Thankfully those fears were ultimately proved to be misplaced and the treble icon finally put pen to paper on a five-and-a-half year deal late in the evening of January 31st, two days before his 27th birthday. Barry Ferguson, twice winner of the Scottish Football Writers' Player of the Year award, had returned to his roots and was finally back where he rightly belonged - wearing the blue of Glasgow Rangers.

Although missing from the starting line-up for the CIS Cup semi-final clash with Dundee United at Hampden that midweek, Ferguson received a well deserved hero's ovation from the majority of the 25,000 plus crowd when he took to the field as a substitute in the latter part of the game. When the midfielder finally appeared, with some twenty minutes of play still remaining, the score was 3-1. The fact that, by the final whistle it was 7-1, really does say it all! In a relatively short period of time, Ferguson had more than stamped his authority on the game and had a helping hand in two of the total tally for the night.

Two weeks after being part of the Rangers team that won at Celtic Park for the first time in five years (Barry was the only survivor from the team that last won there in March, 2000), he claimed his first goal, since his return north, in the SPL meeting with Inverness at Ibrox. Needless to say, it was more than just a little bit special. Following Ricksen's high ball over the forward moving Inverness rearguard, Ferguson then beat the offside trap before unleashing a wonderful shot over keeper Brown and into the back of the net.

That was certainly a characteristically top class effort, but his second, scored on an extremely wet Pittodrie surface at the beginning of May as Rangers chased the championship, was just as, if not more, impressive. Shielding the ball wide right whilst waiting for a runner, Prso saw his man and delivered across the penalty area for Fergie, without breaking stride, to crack a precise left foot drive beyond Esson in goal and dramatically open the scoring. The celebrations that followed, perhaps understandably, took him towards Alex McLeish in the manager's technical area.

In some ways, Barry Ferguson never really left Rangers. In all ways, he was back.

## CLUB CAPTAIN

# BARRY FERGUSON

# OFFICIAL

# YOUNG SUPPORTERS

# CLUB

The OYSC is a fantastic supporters club for Rangers fans aged 16 and under. Only official OYSC members have the opportunity to become matchday mascots and lead the team out onto the pitch. Members are also chosen at random to attend exclusive player events such as signing sessions, Q&A sessions and even dinner with a first team player. Every member receives a membership pack that includes, amongst other goodies, OYSC scarf, baseball cap, sweatband as well as both birthday and Christmas cards at the appropriate time of the year.

Other exclusive benefits include free entry to certain SPL home games (with a paying adult), free entry to the Rangers Tour Experience (with a paying adult) and, subject to availability, free entry to under 21 games. Best of all, each and every member is also automatically entered into amazing 'money can't buy' competitions like the following from last season:

## DINNER WITH A PLAYER
### RECOMMEND A FRIEND
Nine-year-old Fraser Wells recommended his younger brother Murray to join the OYSC and the boys were then selected at random to have dinner with Steven Thompson and Bob Malcolm in the famous Blue Room at Ibrox.

## SIGNING SESSION
100 lucky members were chosen at random to attend a signing session with first-team players including Nacho Novo and Michael Ball.

## 22 MASCOTS

Members are chosen at random to be matchday mascots and, with only two places for each home game, the OYSC decided to make this great opportunity available to more youngsters than ever before. When Rangers played UEFA Cup opponents Auxerre at Ibrox, 22 OYSC members were selected to be mascots and received a full Rangers kit, three match tickets as well as a video and photo of their unique experience.

## FLY WITH THE TEAM

Nine-year-old Ronald Paul from Kilmarnock won the trip of a lifetime and, with his dad, joined the team on their charter flight to Holland for the UEFA Cup game with AZ Alkmaar in early December. His exclusive prize included hotel accommodation, match tickets, £100 spending money as well as VIP invitation to a pre-match meal with Rangers Hospitality.

**Ready to join? Just call 0870 600 1972, visit rangers.co.uk or pop into any Rangers shop.**

# I AM A RANGERS LEGEND
## BUT WHO AM I?

Answers on page 62

**1** I was captain of my previous club in Europe before joining Rangers. I scored with a 30 yard free-kick in a January Old Firm clash as well as netting the second goal at Celtic Park on the day that we won the league. Who am I?

**2** My former clubs include Chelsea and Manchester United and I represented my country 84 times. At the end of my last game in Glasgow, the Rangers crowd honoured me with a standing ovation as I stood alone in the centre circle. Who am I?

**3** Never once booked or sent-off, I was the first post-war Ranger to break the 100 goal barrier. Earlier, during the Second World War, I was decorated with the George Medal for gallantry in the Sicilian campaign. Who am I?

**4** Back in the swinging 1960s, I became the first foreign player to score the winning goal in a Scottish Cup Final when my Old Firm strike was enough for Rangers to lift the cup for the 19th time. Who am I?

**5** My first-ever trophy as captain of the side was awarded after a game against a team from a lower division. Also, I am one of the few players to have been named the Football Writers' Player of the Year on two occasions. Who am I?

**6** These days I am manager of another SPL club but some years ago I was club captain and scored Rangers' only goal of the game when we won our first league title in nine years. Who am I?

**7** I signed from Airdrie and returned there after six years at Ibrox as a part-time player. Known to the fans as the 'Wee Prime Minister' - I scored twice on my October debut. Who am I?

**8** Never on a losing cup final team, I scored six times in those seven Hampden games and was one of the very first Scottish players to wear lightweight continental boots. I was also a member of the Rangers side that became the first British team to reach the final of a European competition. Who am I?

**9** One of my previous clubs was Fiorentina in Italy and both my brother and I played for our country when crowned European champions. In a famous Scottish Cup Final, I scored twice and created all the other Rangers goals that day. Who am I?

**10** In the season that I claimed 34 goals in the league, Rangers' 100th of the championship campaign also had my name on it. I also won the first of my two European awards that year. Who am I?

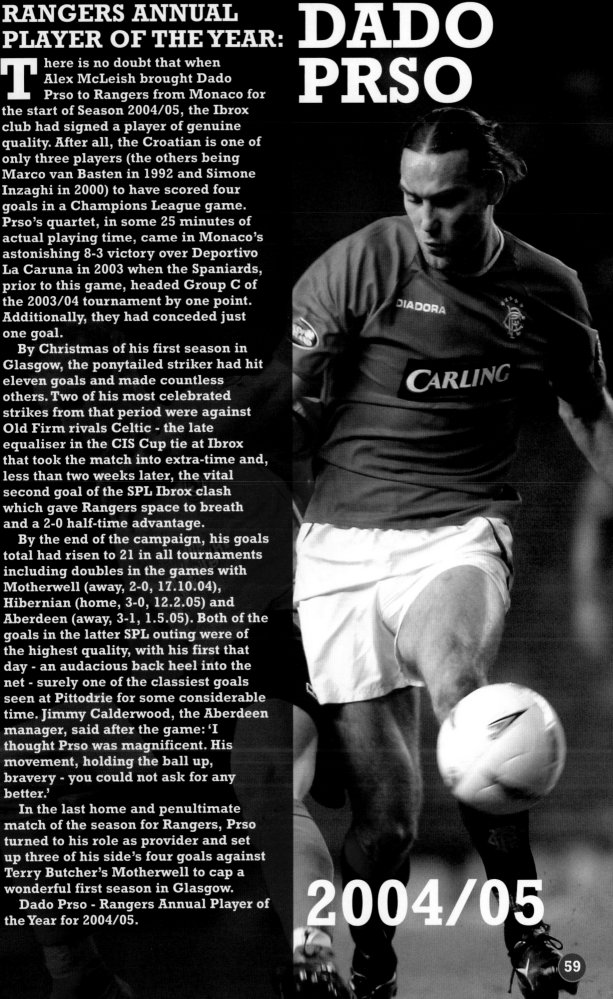

# RANGERS ANNUAL PLAYER OF THE YEAR: DADO PRSO

There is no doubt that when Alex McLeish brought Dado Prso to Rangers from Monaco for the start of Season 2004/05, the Ibrox club had signed a player of genuine quality. After all, the Croatian is one of only three players (the others being Marco van Basten in 1992 and Simone Inzaghi in 2000) to have scored four goals in a Champions League game. Prso's quartet, in some 25 minutes of actual playing time, came in Monaco's astonishing 8-3 victory over Deportivo La Caruna in 2003 when the Spaniards, prior to this game, headed Group C of the 2003/04 tournament by one point. Additionally, they had conceded just one goal.

By Christmas of his first season in Glasgow, the ponytailed striker had hit eleven goals and made countless others. Two of his most celebrated strikes from that period were against Old Firm rivals Celtic - the late equaliser in the CIS Cup tie at Ibrox that took the match into extra-time and, less than two weeks later, the vital second goal of the SPL Ibrox clash which gave Rangers space to breath and a 2-0 half-time advantage.

By the end of the campaign, his goals total had risen to 21 in all tournaments including doubles in the games with Motherwell (away, 2-0, 17.10.04), Hibernian (home, 3-0, 12.2.05) and Aberdeen (away, 3-1, 1.5.05). Both of the goals in the latter SPL outing were of the highest quality, with his first that day - an audacious back heel into the net - surely one of the classiest goals seen at Pittodrie for some considerable time. Jimmy Calderwood, the Aberdeen manager, said after the game: 'I thought Prso was magnificent. His movement, holding the ball up, bravery - you could not ask for any better.'

In the last home and penultimate match of the season for Rangers, Prso turned to his role as provider and set up three of his side's four goals against Terry Butcher's Motherwell to cap a wonderful first season in Glasgow.

Dado Prso - Rangers Annual Player of the Year for 2004/05.

# 2004/05

# QUIZ ANSWERS

## 2004/2005 Season Quiz
1. Nobody - at Pittodrie, their first game ended 0-0.
2. Five - Vignal, Boumsong, Rae, Novo and Prso.
3. Ibrox - as 30,000 celebrated a rather special early evening homecoming!
4. Aberdeen, 31.10.04.
5. Both scored by substitutes - Prso and Arveladze.
6. An astonishing seven.
7. False - it was twice (Hibernian and Dunfermline).
8. Hearts (3-2, 28.11.04).
9. Gregory Vignal and Nacho Novo.
10. Shota Arveladze and Thomas Buffel.

## Scorer Against Celtic Crossword
1. Erik Bo Andersen
2. Paul Gascoigne
3. Maurice Johnston
4. Barry Ferguson
5. Peter Lovenkrands
6. Neil McCann
7. Rod Wallace
8. Brian Laudrup
9. Davie Meiklejohn
10. Ally McCoist

## So you think you know Rangers
1. Colin Stein and Willie Johnston (2).
2. False, it was three - 1961, 1967 and 1972.
3. The Loving Cup.
4. Rangers 3 Celtic 2
5. 101,000.
6. Moses McNeil.
7. Alan Morton.
8. Jock Wallace, 1972-1978 and 1983-1986.
9. Mols, Caniggia, Arveladze, de Boer, Thompson and Arteta.
10. George Young.

## Spot the Difference

## Spot the Ball

## Who Said that Last Season
1. Dado Prso before the April 2005 game against Dunfermline at East End Park.
2. Jean-Alain Boumsong in April 2005.
3. Ian Durrant, after his return to Ibrox as a coach, speaking about the career-threatening injury he sustained at Pittodrie in October, 1988.
4. Maurice Ross talking about the opening goal on CIS Cup final day at Hampden.
5. Fernando Ricksen's reaction to his inclusion in the SPFA Player of the Year shortlist of four.
6. Alex Rae speaking about his days as a Rangers apprentice.
7. Barry Ferguson at the end of the 1-1 drawn game with Caley Thistle at Ibrox.
8. Alex McLeish after Fernando Ricksen was struck by a cigarette lighter at Celtic Park.
9. Former manager Dick Advocaat speaking about goalkeeper Ronald Waterreus.
10. Barry Ferguson after re-signing for Rangers in January 2005.

## Guess Who
1. Nacho Novo
2. Fernando Ricksen
3. Barry Ferguson
4. Stefan Klos

## Alex's Team Talk
1. Nacho Novo (April 2005)
2. Stefan Klos (January 2005)
3. Bob Malcolm (December 2004)
4. Barry Ferguson (February 2005)
5. Alex Rae (November 04)
6. Thomas Buffel (January 2005)
7. Michael Ball (February 2005)
8. Sotirios Kyrgiakos (January 2005)
9. Fernando Ricksen (November 2004)
10. Dado Prso (October 04)

## I am a Rangers Legend – But Who Am I?
1. Jorg Albertz
2. Ray Wilkins
3. Willie Thornton
4. Kai Johansen
5. Barry Ferguson
6. Terry Butcher
7. Ian McMillan
8. Ralph Brand
9. Brian Laudrup
10. Ally McCoist